Published by Ice House Books

Copyright © 2019 Ice House Books

Written by Zulekha Afzal & Raphaella Thompson
Edited by Samantha Rigby
Designed by Joe Brown
Photography credits overleaf

Ice House Books is an imprint of Half Moon Bay Limited
The Ice House, 124 Walcot Street, Bath, BA1 5BG
www.icehousebooks.co.uk

ISBN 978-1-912867-06-6

Printed in China

Potent
Potions

ICE HOUSE BOOKS

PHOTOGRAPHY

CONTENTS

Dragon Heart

Ingredients

* 1 shot lemon flavoured rum
* 2 shots soda water
* ½ tbsp grenadine syrup
* 1 ice cube-size chunk of dry ice, or smaller

Method

1 Mix the rum and soda water in a glass.

2 Add the grenadine and combine.

3 With tongs, add the food-grade dry ice to the glass and serve immediately for the full effect.

DARK FOREST

INGREDIENTS

- ¾ shot freshly squeezed lemon juice
- 6 large blackberries
- ice
- 1½ shots gin
- ½ shot crème de cassis
- ½ shot simple syrup
- black cocktail rimming sugar to decorate

METHOD

1 Combine the fresh lemon juice and blackberries in a glass and mix until the blackberries are broken up. Fill the glass with ice.

2 In a cocktail shaker, combine the gin, crème de cassis and simple syrup by stirring them together.

3 Add the combined gin, crème de cassis and simple syrup to the fresh lemon and blackberry mixture.

4 Stir again and garnish with any leftover blackberries.

5 You can also rim the glass with black rimming sugar for an extra moody effect.

Fire Of The Phoenix

Ingredients

- 1 shot Campari
- 1 shot sweet vermouth
- 1 shot mezcal
- ice
- orange twist to serve

Method

1 Combine the Campari, sweet vermouth and mezcal in a pint glass.

2 Fill the glass with ice and stir.

3 Strain the cocktail into an ice-filled rocks glass.

4 Rub the orange zest around the rim of the glass and garnish with an orange twist.

Top Tip

If you love a bit of showmanship, pour the highest proof alcohol onto a spoon and ignite it, then carefully pour it into your glass for a flaming awesome cocktail.

Calm
Illusions

Ingredients

- 2¼ shots vodka
- 1½ shots coffee
  flavoured liqueur
- 1 tbsp of cream
- ice

Method

1 Dig out your old
  fashioned glass.

2 Pour the vodka and coffee
  flavoured liqueur over ice.

3 Top with cream and stir.

ELECTRIC SPELL

INGREDIENTS

* ice
* 1 shot blue vodka
* 2 shots lemonade
* lemon slices to serve

METHOD

1 Fill a glass about halfway
  full with ice cubes.

2 Pour in the vodka
  and lemonade.

3 Stir in the glass to combine.

4 Serve with sliced lemon.
  It's that easy!

BLACK MAGIC

INGREDIENTS

- 1 shot vodka
- 1 shot white vermouth
- 1¼ shot freshly squeezed lemon juice
- ½ shot simple syrup
- beans from ¼ vanilla pod
- ½ tsp activated charcoal
- ice
- soda water
- lemon wheel to serve

METHOD

1 Pour the vodka, white vermouth and lemon juice into a cocktail shaker, then add the simple syrup, vanilla beans and activated charcoal.

2 Fill the shaker with ice until it's ¾ full and give it a shake.

3 Double strain the cocktail over ice and top up with soda water.

4 Garnish the glass with a lemon wheel.

TOP TIP

Be careful not to add too much charcoal – although it's tasteless, it can leave you with a chalky mouth, even after being strained twice.

THE BITTER TRUTH

INGREDIENTS

Rosemary simple syrup:

- 140 ml (5 fl oz) water
- 9 tbsp of caster sugar
- 2 sprigs of rosemary

Cocktail:

- 2 shots gin
- 5 shots grapefruit juice
- 1 shot rosemary syrup
- ice
- rosemary sprigs to serve
- grapefruit slices to serve

METHOD

For the rosemary simple syrup:

1 Put all of the ingredients into a saucepan and bring to the boil.

2 Turn down the heat and allow the mixture to simmer for three minutes, then turn off the heat and let it sit for five minutes.

3 Strain and discard the rosemary leaves, then leave the syrup to cool.

For the cocktail:

1 Combine the gin, grapefruit juice and rosemary syrup, with a scoop of ice, in a shaker.

2 Fill a tumbler with ice. Strain the cocktail into the glass.

3 Garnish with fresh rosemary and grapefruit slices.

WILD ENCHANTMENT

INGREDIENTS *(20 servings)*

- 6–8 freshly picked elderflower heads
- 500 ml (17.6 fl oz) gin
- 1 strip lemon peel
- 1 tbsp caster/ golden caster sugar
- ice
- tonic water or lemonade
- fresh elderflower to serve
- lemon slices to serve

METHOD

1 Place the elderflower heads, ideally just the blooms, into a large jar.

2 Add the gin, lemon peel and sugar to the jar. Cover and leave the contents to infuse for 24 hours.

3 After the 24 hours, strain the liquid. The infused gin will keep for approximately one month.

4 Pour a shot of the infused gin over ice and top up with tonic water or lemonade.

5 Garnish the glass with a lemon slice and fresh elderflower.

Liquid Gold

Ingredients (*15 servings*)

- 2 litres (70.4 fl oz) traditional cider
- 6 cloves
- 3–4 star anise
- 1 cinnamon stick
- 1 vanilla pod, halved
- ¼ nutmeg, finely grated
- 1 orange, juice of
- 2 clementines, juice of
- 1 pomegranate, juice and seeds of
- 4–5 tbsp caster sugar
- cinnamon stick to serve
- star anise to serve

Method

1 Pour the cider into a large pan. Keep it on a low heat and let it warm through for a few minutes.

2 Add all of the spices and juices then turn the heat up slightly.

3 Once the mixture is boiling, turn it down to a simmer and leave it for 5–8 minutes to allow everything to infuse.

4 Once you've tasted your mulled cider, add sugar to taste.

5 Serve with a cinnamon stick and star anise in the glass.

POISONOUS TOUCH

INGREDIENTS

- 1 shot blood orange flavoured vodka
- ½ shot orange liqueur
- 2 shots pomegranate juice
- ice
- chilled champagne
- 1 tbsp pomegranate seeds to serve
- blood orange slice to serve
- rosemary sprig to serve

METHOD

1 Pour the vodka, orange liqueur and pomegranate juice into a glass over ice, then stir.

2 Top the glass with chilled champagne to taste.

3 Garnish with pomegranate seeds, an orange slice and rosemary.

WITCHES' BREW

INGREDIENTS

- 1 shot vodka
- 1 shot coconut rum
- ½ shot blue curacao
- ½ shot pineapple juice
- 1 ice cube-size chunk of dry ice, or smaller

METHOD

1 Add the vodka, rum, curacao and pineapple juice to a cocktail shaker and shake well.

2 Strain the mix into a glass.

3 To add a little extra magic, use tongs to add the food-grade dry ice to the glass and serve immediately.

PUMPKIN PREDICTIONS

INGREDIENTS

- 2 shots bourbon
- 1 shot maple syrup
- ½ shot orange flavoured liqueur
- 2 tbsp pumpkin purée
- 1 dash orange bitters

METHOD

1 Fill a cocktail shaker with ice,
  the bourbon, maple syrup,
  orange flavoured liqueur,
  pumpkin purée and bitters.

2 Shake the mixture well and
  strain it into a glass over ice
  or into shot glasses.

Sunset Conjurings

Ingredients *(4–6 servings)*

- 750 ml (26.4 fl oz) bottle red wine
- 1 lemon, cut into wedges
- 1 orange, cut into wedges
- 2 shots brandy
- 2 tbsp sugar
- 480 ml (16.9 fl oz) ginger ale or soda water
- ice
- orange slices to serve
- apple slices to serve

Method

1 Pour the wine into a large pitcher and squeeze in the juice from the lemon and orange wedges.

2 Add the fruit wedges (without seeds if possible) to the wine. Add the brandy and sugar then stir gently until the sugar has dissolved.

3 Cover the pitcher and chill it in the fridge overnight or for eight hours to let all of the flavours infuse.

4 Add the ginger ale or soda water before serving.

5 Pour into a glass over ice and serve with the orange and apple slices.

BLACK WIDOW

INGREDIENTS

- 2 shots vodka
- 1 shot blue curacao
- ½ shot black raspberry liqueur
- orange twist to serve

METHOD

1 Pour the vodka, blue curacao
  and black raspberry liqueur
  into a cocktail shaker with ice.

2 Shake the cocktail well
  then strain it into a chilled
  martini glass.

3 Garnish the glass with
  an orange zest twist.

Smoking Amber

Ingredients

- 2 shots rum
- ½ shot orange flavoured liqueur
- 120 ml (4.2 fl oz) sparkling pomegranate juice
- 1 ice cube-size chunk of dry ice, or smaller
- orange twist to serve

Method

1. Add the rum and orange flavoured liqueur to a shaker, then shake well and strain into a glass.

2. Top up the glass with sparkling pomegranate juice.

3. With tongs, add the food-grade dry ice to the glass.

4. Garnish the glass with an orange zest twist.

BEWITCHING BRAMBLE

INGREDIENTS

Blackberry syrup:

- 100 g (3.5 oz) white caster sugar
- 100 ml (3.5 fl oz) water
- 1 tbsp blackberries

Cocktail:

- 2 shots sloe gin
- 1 shot gin
- 1 shot lemon juice
- ice, crushed
- blackberries to serve

METHOD

For the blackberry syrup:

1 Put the sugar in a small saucepan and add the water and blackberries.

2 Bring the mixture to the boil then take it off the heat and gently squash the blackberries.

3 Leave the syrup to cool then strain into a bottle or jar.

For the cocktail:

1 Pour the sloe gin, gin, lemon juice and two teaspoons of the blackberry syrup into a cocktail shaker with ice in.

2 Shake well then strain the cocktail into a glass filled with crushed ice.

3 Garnish with fresh blackberries.

Evening Alchemy

Ingredients

- ½ shot lime juice
- ice, crushed
- 2 shots vodka
- cold ginger beer to taste
- cranberries to serve
- lime peel to serve

Method

1 Pour the lime juice into a mug.

2 Add some ice and pour in the vodka, then top up the mug with cold ginger beer.

3 Gently stir the cocktail.

4 Garnish with a fresh cranberry wrapped in a strip of lime peel, on a cocktail stick.

STAR DUST

INGREDIENTS

- 2 shots vodka
- 1 shot freshly brewed espresso
- ½ shot coffee liqueur
- ½ shot simple syrup
- edible gold glitter to decorate
- mint leaf to serve

METHOD

1. Pour the vodka, espresso, coffee liqueur and simple syrup into a shaker with ice.

2. Shake well and strain into a chilled cocktail glass.

3. Decorate with a dusting of edible gold glitter and garnish with a mint leaf.

DREAMY DEVILRY

INGREDIENTS *(4–5 servings)*

Thyme simple syrup:

- 7 tbsp sugar
- 120 ml (4.2 fl oz) water
- 6 thyme sprigs

Cocktail:

- 2 plums
- 1¼ shot lemon juice
- ice, crushed
- 1 bottle Prosecco
- thyme sprigs to serve
- plum slices to serve

METHOD

For the thyme simple syrup:

1 Pour the sugar and water into a pan and bring to the boil.

2 Remove the syrup from the heat and add the thyme sprigs, then gently stir the syrup and allow it to cool.

For the cocktail:

1 Peel and chop two plums then add them and the lemon juice to the syrup mixture. Mix together until the plum juices are released.

2 Shake well with ice in a shaker, then pour over crushed ice.

3 Top up the glass with Prosecco and garnish with fresh plum slices and thyme sprigs.

MOONSTONE

INGREDIENTS

- 2 shots vodka
- ½ shot dry vermouth
- 1 tsp blue curacao
- 1 tsp fresh lemon juice
- 1 ice cube-size chunk
  of dry ice, or smaller

METHOD

1 Combine the vodka, dry
  vermouth, blue curacao
  and lemon juice in a cocktail
  shaker with some ice.

2 Shake well then strain the
  cocktail into a martini class.

3 Add the food-grade dry
  ice using tongs and serve
  immediately.

Red Allure

Ingredients

- 1 tbsp pomegranate seeds
- 1 shot vodka
- cranberry and pomegranate juice to taste
- dry ginger ale to taste
- ice
- edible fake blood to rim the glass

Method

1. Put the pomegranate seeds into the bottom of the glass.

2. Pour in the vodka and the cranberry and pomegranate juice, then top up the glass with ginger ale.

3. Gently stir the cocktail and add some ice.

4. Rim the glass with edible fake blood for an extra blood thirsty touch.

Sunset Hour

Ingredients

- 1 shot light rum
- 1 shot dark rum
- 1 shot apricot liqueur
- 2 shots orange juice
- 1 dash lime bitters
- ice, crushed
- ½ shot 151 rum
- orange slice to serve
- mint leaves to serve

Method

1 Pour the light rum, dark rum, apricot liqueur, orange juice and lime bitters into a cocktail shaker.

2 Shake well then pour the cocktail into a glass filled with crushed ice.

3 Add the 151 rum to the cocktail.

4 Garnish the cocktail with an orange slice and mint leaves.

MIDNIGHT MAGIC

INGREDIENTS

- 2 shots vodka
- ½ shot coffee liqueur
- ice
- coca-cola to taste (optional)
- cinnamon stick to serve
- glace cherry to serve

METHOD

1 Add the vodka and coffee liqueur
to a mixing glass filled with ice,
then stir.

2 Strain into a glass filled with ice.

3 Top up with coca-cola to taste.

4 Serve with a cinnamon stick
and glace cherry.

WINTER'S STORM

- 1 bottle of red wine
- brandy to taste
- 2–3 tbsp brown sugar
- 2 oranges, sliced into wheels
- handful of dried cranberries
- small piece of ginger (approx. 2 inches), peeled and finely sliced
- 2 cinnamon sticks, broken up with a little extra to serve
- star anise to serve

METHOD

1 Pour the wine and brandy into a large pan.

2 Gently stir in the sugar, orange slices, dried cranberries, ginger and cinnamon sticks.

3 Heat gently for 3–4 minutes or until the sugar has dissolved (be careful not to bring the mixture to the boil).

4 Ladle the mulled wine into the glasses and serve with cinnamon sticks and star anise.

SUNLIGHT SORCERY

INGREDIENTS

- 2 shots vanilla vodka
- ½ shot cream liqueur
- ½ shot pumpkin liqueur or pumpkin spice syrup
- black cocktail rimming sugar to decorate

METHOD

1. Fill a cocktail shaker with ice and pour in the vodka and cream liqueur.

2. Shake well then add the pumpkin liqueur or pumpkin spice syrup.

3. Shake again before straining the cocktail into a chilled martini glass.

4. Garnish the rim of the glass with black rimming sugar.

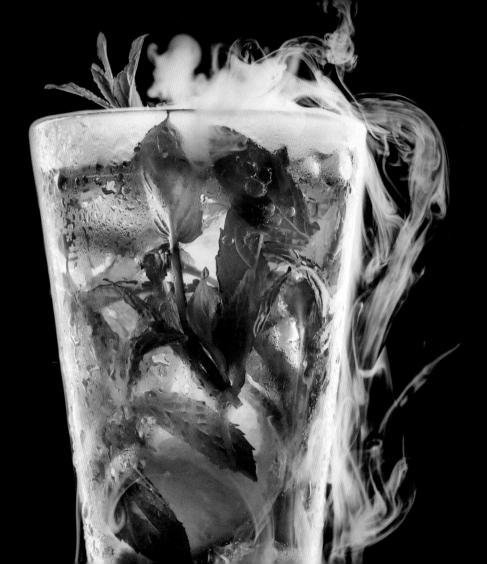

Whimsical Wizardry

Ingredients

- ¼ lemon, cut into 2 wedges
- ¼ lime, cut into 2 wedges
- 2 tbsp sugar, or to taste
- mint leaves
- ice

- 2 shots white rum
- soda water to taste
- 1 ice cube-size chunk of dry ice, or smaller

Method

1. In a glass, muddle together the lemon and lime wedges with the sugar.

2. Rub the mint leaves around the rim of the glass then pop them into the glass. Push the mint down into the juice using a muddler or long handled spoon.

3. Add some ice and pour in the rum. Gently stir the cocktail together until the sugar dissolves.

4. Top up the glass with soda water.

5. Add the food-grade dry ice using tongs and serve immediately.

DRY ICE CARE INSTRUCTIONS

While dry ice looks great when added to your cocktails, there are a few things you should be aware of before handling it.

- *Never ingest dry ice or place it in your mouth.*

- *Never let dry ice touch your skin (always use gloves or tongs when adding it to your cocktails).*

- *Never store or handle dry ice in enclosed areas.*

- *Never serve a drink with dry ice without letting the recipient know it's there.*

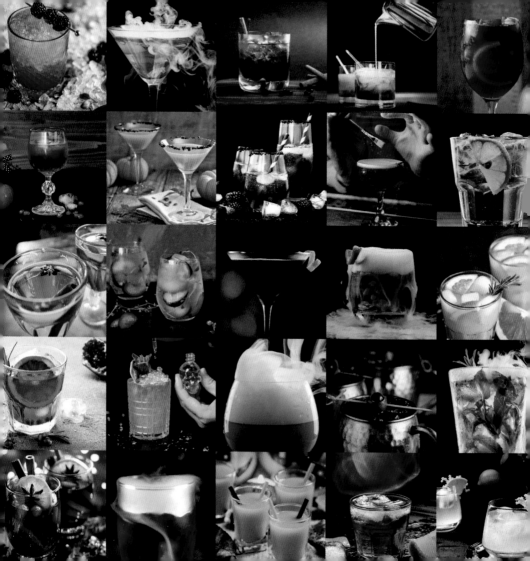